STEVEN BARTLETT

A Detailed Life Story

John Brooklyn

Table of Contents

INTRODUCTION

Introducing the extraordinary personality behind the crème de la crème of podcasts in the UK, *The Diary of a CEO* is none other than Steven Bartlett. He's not just the average personality. He's an entrepreneur, speaker, investor, author, and an explorer of the hidden depths of the lives of the world's leading experts and thinkers.

Now, let's dive into Steven's impressive investment portfolio. This guy knows a thing or two about the health and wellness industry. He's thrown some serious cash into *Zoe*, a specialized nutrition program crafted by the world's leading experts. He's also backed Huel, the UK's fastest-growing e-commerce startup.

Steven's investment prowess extends far beyond the realm of health and wellness. He's dabbled in companies like AbCellera, Atai Life Sciences, and Alto Neuroscience. He is all about cutting-edge technologies and groundbreaking ideas. Blockchain, biotech, outer space, Web 3.0, and social media are just a few of his investing priorities.

Steven is a visionary entrepreneur who has left an indelible mark on the business world. As a co-founder of *Flight Story*, a distinguished marketing and communications firm, he has revolutionized the field of social media promotion with his groundbreaking ideas and innovative methods. Steven's unparalleled expertise has made *Flight Story* the go-to partner for top-tier businesses seeking unparalleled success.

Not content with just one venture, Steven has also established *Flight Company*, a private equity firm dedicated to propelling the next wave of European unicorns. With his astute business acumen, Steven is driving the growth and success of promising startups, ensuring their ascent to greatness.

Furthermore, Steven's influence extends to the realm of technology. As a co-founder of *thirdweb*, a cutting-edge software platform, he has simplified the development of web3 apps, garnering support from industry giants like Shopify and Coinbase.

The trailblazer has penned a book that defied convention with its satirical title, *"Happy Millionaire."* This audacious masterpiece skyrocketed to the top of The Sunday Times best-seller list, solidifying Steven's status as a literary luminary.

Breaking barriers and shattering glass ceilings, Steven became the youngest investor ever to grace the esteemed Dragons Den panel on the beloved BBC show.

Recognizing his exceptional contributions, Steven was bestowed with the prestigious British Black Entrepreneur of the Year award. Rather than basking in the glory of this accolade, he selflessly redirected his focus toward uplifting underprivileged schools and communities. His dedication aimed to ignite the spark of inspiration within the hearts of the next generation of BAME entrepreneurs and creatives.

Ever the catalyst for change, Steven embarked on a groundbreaking endeavor to empower juvenile detainees under the care of His Majesty's Prison Service. Collaborating with these young souls, he harnessed their in-cell technology to disseminate *The Diary of a CEO* podcast.

Through this innovative initiative, he aimed to educate and motivate, offering a glimmer of hope in the darkest of places.

His indomitable spirit and commitment to excellence did not go unnoticed. The *Powerlist,* a revered compilation of the UK's most influential individuals of African, African Caribbean, and African American descent, proudly featured him in its latest edition. This recognition solidified his place among the nation's powerhouses.

But it is not just the elite who are captivated by Steven's magnetic aura. His followers span a diverse spectrum, ranging from budding company owners to visionary artists, from soul-stirring musicians to astute executives. They are drawn to his wisdom, his charisma, and his ability to inspire greatness within each and every one of them.

His visionary approach has paved the way for seamless and efficient app development, empowering businesses to thrive in the digital age.

IN BOTSWANA

Born on August 26, 1992, in the land of Botswana, Africa, Steven Bartlett emerged into this world. Hailing from a lineage rooted in Britain, he moved to Plymouth when he was two years with both of his parents. He is the fourth and youngest child to his Nigerian mother and British Father. While his mother's education ended abruptly at the age of seven without learning to read or write, on the other hand, his father thrived as a successful structural engineer.

However, the road to success was not paved with gold for young Steven, as his family faced arduous financial challenges during his formative years.

In the face of adversity, Steven's invincible spirit shone through. He was an insecure boy who struggled in school, barely scraping through his GCSEs and A-levels. However, his attention was often diverted towards other endeavors including such as arranging school trips, making agreements with vending machine companies, and earning a profit from those transactions. It became evident at a young age that his true passion and aptitude were aligned with the field of entrepreneurship.

With an unswerving entrepreneurial mindset, defying the odds imposed by his disadvantaged background. Driven by an insatiable hunger for success, he was determined to transcend his circumstances and make an indelible impact on the world.

Growing up in the rugged landscapes of Yorkshire, England, Steven's upbringing forged him into a tenacious and diligent individual. It was here that he honed the qualities that would shape him into the ambitious and hardworking man he would ultimately become.

Unyielding in his pursuit of greatness, Steven made a pivotal decision that would alter the course of his life. After relocating to Manchester to seek an academic path in Business Management at Manchester Metropolitan University, he resolved that traditional education was not the path for him. His entrepreneurial endeavors overshadowed his desire to continue with his studies. With an audacious leap of faith, he charted his own course, venturing into uncharted territories.

Consequently, it led to a disagreement with his parents, especially his mother. His mother was devastated because she believed Bartlett had wasted his educational opportunities, which she never had when she was growing up.

Since his early adulthood, Steven has been captivated by the immense potential of social media in propelling careers and shaping personal identities. He possesses a profound comprehension of the profound impact wielded by platforms such as Facebook, Twitter, Instagram, and YouTube. Driven by his fascination, he embarked on a journey into the realm of social media marketing and brand development, skillfully crafting and disseminating compelling content across these influential channels.

PROFESSIONAL JOURNEY

Small Beginnings

From a tender age, Steven Bartlett began an incredible odyssey as a businessperson, driven by an innate desire to transcend his modest origins in Yorkshire, England. Although the specifics of his initial business ventures remain somewhat elusive, it is widely known that he fearlessly dabbled in various entrepreneurial pursuits during his teenage years. Even in his youth, Steven exhibited an exceptional acumen for business in the realm of online networking. Recognizing the immense potential of social media as a powerful advertising platform and a catalyst for personal branding, he astutely grasped its unparalleled ability to forge connections between individuals and corporations.

Steven Bartlett's entrepreneurial spirit shone brightly as he embarked on his journey of establishing a tutoring firm during his teenage years. Amidst the whirlwind of adolescence, he pursued this venture, driven by a burning desire to share his knowledge and empower others to achieve educational excellence. He guided students across various subjects, providing them with invaluable academic support and guidance.

However, Steven Bartlett's thirst for success did not stop there. Having conquered the teaching realm, he ventured into the event management industry, showcasing his versatility and adaptability. With his newly formed company, he masterfully orchestrated a diverse array of events, ranging from intimate gatherings to extravagant galas. Through this endeavor, he undoubtedly honed his skills in project management, customer service, and marketing, gaining invaluable expertise.

Bartlett's commercial aptitude was greatly influenced by his early endeavors. As a young entrepreneur, he encountered real-world challenges, honed his creative problem-solving skills, and acquired invaluable experience. The triumphs he achieved in the realm of digital marketing and social media, working with renowned firms such as *Social Chain*, can be directly attributed to the lessons he gleaned from his early ventures.

The Story Behind Social Chain

When Steven Bartlett, then 19 years old, came up with the idea for *Wallpark* in 2012, he envisioned a digital firm. The whole idea started when he was at Manchester Metropolitan University. While studying Business Management, he quickly realized his passion for creating a social media platform that connects university students with similar interests in the same city. He envisioned this platform, called *Wallpark,* as a place where students could share information, advertise events, and sell items like textbooks. To fully dedicate himself to this project, Bartlett decided to drop out of university.

Despite having no initial investment, he hustled by sleeping on the streets and using Wi-Fi in cafes. After successfully establishing *Wallpark*, he left to do consultancy work for clients in social media. Social media marketing, content production, and influencer outreach were among the primary areas of focus for *Wallpark*. *Wallpark*'s mission revolved around offering innovative solutions for businesses to effectively engage with their core consumers through the vast reach of social media. Recognizing the ever-increasing significance of social media marketing, *Wallpark* seized the opportunity to tap into its target demographic as the digital landscape evolved and the influence of social media continued to surge.

During his research, Bartlett discovered the behavior of young people on social media, particularly *Twitter,* and came across a Twitter page created by a student named Dominic McGregor, which was attracting a large number of followers with funny and relatable student content. Bartlett saw the potential to connect brands with their audiences through these platforms without sacrificing engagement or following. He reached out to McGregor and shared his vision, and McGregor also decided to leave his studies.

In 2014, they founded *Social Chain, a company* formed with a focus on reaching and engaging millennials across several social media channels. The firm targeted the increasingly important millennial and Gen Z markets with data-driven insights and innovative techniques. *Social Chain* was created to assist Unii with social promotion and influencer engagement for their student social platform. It received £300,000 in seed funding and has now raised over £1m. Its current revenue reads at EUR 58.4 million.

Dominic contributed his knowledge in advertising and creative planning. Along with Bartlett, he was instrumental in *Social Chain*'s rise to prominence and helped drive the company's success.

Social Chain's first client, the gaming app *Tippy Tap*, wanted to increase app downloads. Despite the uncertainty, they launched a campaign and achieved outstanding results. *Tippy Tap* reached the top of the app store rankings for weeks and even garnered media attention from the BBC. This success marked a significant breakthrough for *Social Chain*.

In just two short years, this company has emerged as one of Europe's most influential marketing agencies. Their unparalleled success has been recognized through numerous prestigious awards, including the esteemed title of The Drums Social Media Marketing Agency of the

Year. Collaborating with renowned brands such as *Spotify, Microsoft, and Comedy Central,* they cater to these brands' campaigns by transforming mere concepts into awe-inspiring campaigns.

Fueling their meteoric rise, this company secured a substantial investment from the esteemed German media powerhouse, *Glow Media.* This strategic partnership has not only propelled their expansion into new and exciting markets like Germany and the United States but has also solidified their position as industry trailblazers. It also attracted top brands as *Glow Artists*, a subsidiary of *Glow Media* worked with companies like McDonald's, the BBC, and Nintendo.

While boasting multiple offices across various locations, it is their headquarters in the vibrant city of Manchester that truly captivates. Within these walls are an array of amenities that redefine the concept of a workplace. It has a slide, a ball pit, a fully stocked bar, table tennis, and a puppy park. Before then, they were just young dropouts sharing a small flat in London.

In 2019, the Manchester-based Social Chain Group successfully did a reverse merger with the German online retailer Lumaland, marking its first public listing and establishing a powerful and unified advertising entity valued at €186m.

Reverse mergers also referred to as reverse takeovers, have emerged as a favored option for companies seeking to secure capital. This strategic maneuver involves a private company (Social Chain) assuming control of a publicly traded company (Lumaland), thereby transforming itself into a publicly traded entity. As part of this process, the shareholders of the private company obtain substantial ownership in the newly established public company and wield influence over its board of directors. Ultimately, the private and public entities merge, culminating in the formation of a unified organization that is publicly traded.

Lumaland, renowned for its expertise in beanbags and mattresses, reported impressive revenues of €90m ($100m) in 2018. This strategic move was widely regarded as a potential game-changer in the industry, as it brought together an advertising agency with a brand that offers tangible products. With a clear vision to expand its external revenue streams, the newly merged firm set its sights on reaching an astounding 1.8 billion customers. This ambitious goal showcased the company's determination to leverage its combined strengths and capitalize on the vast market potential. The merger also signaled the emergence of a new breed of integrated agency, one that prioritizes creativity while seamlessly integrating commercial interests.

Under the new name Lumaland/Social Chain AG, the company relocated its headquarters to Berlin while maintaining a strong presence in northwest England. The Social Chain co-founder Steve Bartlett continued the role of co-CEO alongside Holger Hansen and Wanja Sören Oberhof, ensuring a seamless transition and continuity in leadership. Additionally, the highly respected Dr. Georg Kofler, renowned for his founding of ProSieben and Premiere in Germany, took on the role of chairman, owning an impressive 47% stake in the company.

The significance of this merger was further underscored by the company's listing on the prestigious Prime Standard of the Frankfurt Stock Exchange in mid-2020. The merger also led to the company's change of name from Social Chain to Social Chain AG.

After the merger, Social Chain embarked on an acquisition spree, securing a majority stake in KoRo, an online superfoods retailer, as well as Solidmind, a supplements supplier, Urbanara, a natural interior brand company, Conteam: below, a German digital marketing agency, and drtv.agency, an advertising agency. In May 2020, the company made its most significant acquisition, obtaining a 51% stake in A4D Inc, a renowned digital performance marketing agency based in California.

By the end of 2019, Bartlett disclosed on Twitter that Social Chain AG had successfully completed the acquisition of over 30 companies, encompassing five to ten marketing agencies and approximately 20 e-commerce businesses.

Sadly, Bartlett left the company in December 2020 relinquishing his role as a director in the company. He left after suggesting the separation of the marketing and e-commerce sides, which was rejected by the board. His resignation left uncertainty regarding whether he maintained shares in the company and would gain from potential future sales.

At the beginning of 2023, it was revealed that its rival, the social and digital media group, Brave Bison, had successfully negotiated an agreement to acquire the company with an initial payment of £7.7m with the potential to pay more if certain earnings goals are met. The buyer expects the acquisition to increase their social media advertising revenues to £15m for the year. According to Business-live.co.uk, the company's sale will not result in any financial gain for Mr. Bartlett and Mr. McGregor, as they have no remaining equity interest in it. Following the agreement, the merger between Brave Bison and Social Chain will result in an enlarged social media advertising practice, with Metcalfe taking on the responsibility. The former CEO of Social Chain is quite confident in *Brave Bison*, as a brand being managed by individuals with a strong marketing background.

However, controversy arose after the sale of the Social Chain. It began from the information that was shared on Bartlett's online bio before and after the company was acquired which people found misleading. His bio stated that he stepped down as joint CEO in 2020 leaving the company at a market valuation of $600M. After the acquisition of *Social Chain,* his bio reads a different story. It now states that he stepped down in 2020 and the company achieved a market valuation of over $600 million. When in fact, the company was valued at $620 million when it floated in Frankfurt in October 2021 which was after Bartlett resigned in 2020.

Nevertheless, the dispute resurfaced after the sale of *Social Chain* for £7.7 million. The value for which the company was acquired caused perplexity among those who had recognized the company's earlier projections of nearly £1bn in revenue by 2023's conclusion. A number of entrepreneurs and businessmen also expressed confusion and skepticism about the company's valuation. However, the other CEO of Social Chain, Wanja Sören

Oberhof, defended Bartlett and credited him as being essential to the company's growth.

To clarify the confusion, it is claimed that the brand which was acquired for £7.7 million is different from Social Chain AG which amassed revenues of approximately €241.6m in 2021.

Bartlett stated that Social Chain AG, in his absence, shifted its focus towards the e-commerce aspect of the business. Consequently, a significant portion of the marketing agencies, which accounted for approximately £70m in total revenues, were sold off. He has also made a bid to acquire an agency from Social Chains' portfolio.

Although Steven stepped aside as CEO, his influence and effect on Social Chain AG undoubtedly remained substantial.

Although it is stated that the reason behind Bartlett's resignation was because the board swept off his suggestion of separating the company, there could be other conditions that could have led to his decision.

Here's a more in-depth look at the factors that were responsible for his leaving:

- After heading Social Chain for a while and watching it become a worldwide social media marketing business, Steven who is business driven may have wanted to branch out and try new things.

- Steven's decision to stand down as CEO was part of a planned transition, and not a sudden one.

- Bartlett, a social media influencer and thought leader has a strong personal brand. It is possible that he stepped down as CEO so he could have more time and freedom to devote to building his own brand, producing content, and interacting with his audience.

o One of the implications of his resignation is opening the door for new management at the company. This shift in management may result in the introduction of innovative approaches that would help the organization meet future problems.

The Achievements of Social Chain AG under Bartlett's Leadership

Social Chain AG has grown into a worldwide power in social media marketing because of Bartlett and McGregor's innovative thinking and ability to adapt to new platforms. During Steven Bartlett's tenure as CEO, Social Chain expanded rapidly and set a number of precedent-setting precedents in the field of social media advertising. A fuller summary of the company's development and key achievements follows:

> ➢ The firm rebranded from *Wallpark* to Social Chain and quickly grew to provide more than just digital marketing services. It centered on coming up with creative ways to leverage social media to reach and

interact with millennials and people of the upcoming Generation Z. Brands were able to make genuine connections with young customers via Social Chain's data-driven strategy and innovative marketing.

➢ Under Bartlett's leadership, Social Chain achieved success through influencer marketing. They realized the value of collaborating with popular social media influencers to enhance brand messages. By teaming up with relevant influencers, they effectively reached and connected with their target audience, resulting in increased engagement and brand loyalty for their clients.

➢ Social Chain became known for creating viral campaigns and setting trends on social media. The firm had an in-depth familiarity with internet culture and acted swiftly to cash in on new fads and memes for the advantage of its customers. Consequently, Social Chain was able to anticipate industry shifts and provide outstanding outcomes for companies hoping to build their brands' online profiles.

➢ As part of the company's growth plan, Bartlett made smart acquisitions to increase the company's capabilities and market presence. These acquisitions helped the company expand its capabilities and reach in the market. By acquiring complementary businesses, Social Chain was able to offer a wider range of services to its clients, making it a stronger and more comprehensive social media marketing agency.

33 | P a g e

➢ Social Chain became known for its success in providing innovative marketing solutions to high-profile clients in various industries. The company has worked with globally recognized brands, helping them create impactful campaigns and achieve their marketing goals. This collaboration with reputable clients further cemented Social Chain's reputation in the industry.

➢ After establishing a foothold in the United Kingdom, Social Chain branched out to become a worldwide company. The firm was able to serve a wider range of customers and connect with more people by becoming global.

➢ The company's prominence and notoriety are attributed in part to

Steven Bartlett's role as a thought leader in the fields of entrepreneurship, marketing, and social media. Bartlett's personal status as a social media influencer and his many media appearances boosted Social Chain's reputation and brought in new clients.

➤ Social Chain was recognized and awarded for its groundbreaking marketing initiatives and accomplishments. The company's efforts in social media marketing were recognized with several nominations and awards from the industry.

➤ In 2019, Social Chain's parent business, The Social Chain Group, went public on the London Stock Exchange. This action was a major turning point in Steven Bartlett's career and the company's progress as a marketing powerhouse.

Steven Bartlett, A Brand

Steven Bartlett's personal brand as a social media influencer has had a profound impact on his reputation and influence in the realm of entrepreneurship and marketing. Now, let us delve deeper into the intricacies of his personal brand and explore how he skillfully connected with his audience.

Bartlett's success as a social media influencer may be attributed in large part to his honesty and openness. His audience was able to connect with him on a deeper level because of the personal tales, experiences, and lessons he imparted.

Bartlett gained the trust of his audience by sharing the ups and downs of his own entrepreneurial experience in an honest and forthright manner.

Inspirational and upbeat words were commonplace in Steven Bartlett's social media posts. He urged his listeners to do what they love, to take chances, and to see failure as a necessary part of the learning process. His ability to convey complex ideas in simple terms struck a chord with budding company owners and industry fans looking for inspiration.

As a highly accomplished entrepreneur, Steven Bartlett possesses a vast wealth of knowledge and invaluable insights to offer. He generously imparts valuable tips, strategies, and advice on a wide range of topics including marketing, branding, leadership, and business development. His practical and actionable insights make his content immensely valuable to aspiring entrepreneurs seeking to initiate or expand their ventures.

Bartlett is a skilled storyteller who uses engaging anecdotes to make his points. His narrative skills captivated his audience, whether he was discussing his own business experiences or highlighting the motivational success stories of others. He is quite present in his social media communities. By engaging with his listeners via comments, questions, and conversations, he fosters a feeling of belonging and rapport. This back-and-forth helped create an enthusiastic fan base.

He has successfully established a strong presence on various social media platforms like YouTube, Instagram, Twitter, and LinkedIn. This strategic approach has enabled him to connect with a wide range of individuals, catering his content to suit the unique preferences and behaviors of users on each platform.

As Bartlett's reputation expanded, he teamed up with other successful businesspeople, innovators, and thought leaders. His reputation as a leading figure in the world of business and advertising was bolstered by the exposure he gained via these partnerships.

The Voice Behind the Mic

The *Diary of a CEO* audio series was born out of Steven's decision to step down as CEO of Social Chain AG at the young age of 27. It provides unfiltered insights into success and equips listeners with the knowledge they need to create the life they desire. It also features in-depth interviews with prominent businesspeople who have made significant contributions to culture and achieved greatness. Steven, the host, interviews some of the world's most influential people, experts, and thinkers, delving into their untold truths, and unlearned lessons.

The series aims to provide a raw and emotional perspective, living up to its name by sharing personal experiences and thoughts that are often not openly discussed. These candid conversations offer a level of honesty rarely seen in traditional interviews, providing valuable and relatable content for both Steven and the audience. Over 20 million copies of the series have been downloaded worldwide.

In August 2022, it reached a milestone by exceeding 10 million downloads in a month for the first time. Each month, a total of eight episodes are released, with 60% of their audience coming from the UK and 15% from the US.

According to Spotify data, their audience has an almost equal gender balance. The podcast which is made available on various platforms including *Apple, Amazon, and Spotify,* has distribution agreements with major airlines like British Airways, Qatar Airlines, Aer Lingus, Air Canada, and Iberia. Based on 2022 rankings by *Chartable, The Diary Of A CEO* has emerged as the most downloaded podcast across all audio platforms in Great Britain. Furthermore, the figures provided by Chartable reveal that T*he Diary Of A CEO* is attracting approximately 50,000 new subscribers on YouTube each month.

As a result of his access to influential people through the audio series, he is able to present his audience with insightful interviews and the counsel of those he has interviewed. This has also increased his network of business affiliations and relationships.

The podcast aims to expand its audience globally and provide a safe platform for interesting individuals to share their ideas and experiences. The host also plans on branching out into other podcasts or funding them.

51 Cards:

The Conversation Cards innovated by Steve Bartlett are a collection of 51 thought-provoking questions that are guaranteed to ignite meaningful discussions in any setting. Derived from the tradition of *The Diary of a CEO* podcast, each question is anonymously written by previous guests and carefully selected to inspire raw, honest, and unfiltered conversations like never before.

These cards have been crafted by individuals who have shaped culture, achieved greatness, and created stories worth studying. They are specifically designed to stimulate deep and meaningful dialogue, allowing a person to delve into the depths of their thoughts and emotions.

The versatility of these cards is unparalleled. They can be used as personal journaling prompts to gain a better understanding of a person or as a catalyst for engaging in conversations with friends, family, or even strangers. The possibilities are endless.

From first dates to casual chats with colleagues, The Conversation Cards serve as a powerful tool to bring people closer together. They encourage honesty, reflection, and a deeper understanding of your relationship with yourself and your loved ones. Whether it's a post-dinner party game, a fun activity during a road trip, a source of entertainment on a long-haul flight, or a means to connect during a family reunion, these cards promise to break down barriers and cut through years of superficiality to reach the core of the individuals in your world.

Thirdweb

Bartlett is also one of the visionaries behind *Thirdweb* and *Flight Story*. *Thirdweb*, a startup accelerator, collaborates with aspiring entrepreneurs to transform their ideas into reality. Under Steven Bartlett's leadership, *ThirdWeb* has emerged as a groundbreaking platform that is spearheading the *Web3* revolution. With a substantial investment of $5 million from esteemed individuals like Gary Vaynerchuk, *ThirdWeb* is poised to revolutionize the digital landscape.

Experiencing seamless creation, publication, and maintenance of your Web3 projects is achievable with *ThirdWeb*'s comprehensive suite of tools designed for developers, artists, and entrepreneurs. By leveraging *ThirdWeb*'s user-friendly interface, individuals can effortlessly integrate NFTs, markets, and social tokens into their Web3 applications, without the need for extensive coding knowledge.

With *ThirdWeb*'s help, programmers, designers, and marketers are able to effortlessly construct, execute, and handle a Web3 initiative. This software is not only accessible to all but also completely free, ensuring that individuals from all walks of life can embark on their Web3 journey with ease.

Flight Fund

One of Steven's utmost priorities is to foster the growth of the next generation of Black, Asian, and Latino (BAME) business owners and artists. The Flight Fund serves as a bridge, connecting startups with Europe's most cutting-edge businesses. It focuses its investments on groundbreaking sectors such as blockchain, biotech, health and wellness, commerce, technology, and space. What sets Flight Fund apart is its exclusive support from the trailblazing European entrepreneurs, known as the *Avengers*.

By partnering with Flight Fund, businesses gain unparalleled access to a wealth of expertise and an invaluable network of contacts. This is because the Fund has been meticulously crafted to become Europe's most triumphant private equity fund.

Flight Story

Flight Story is a dynamic communications and marketing firm that seizes the opportunity to position its clients' brands at the forefront of consumer expectations. Co-founded by Bartlett and Oliver Yonchev, *Flight Story* offers a range of services to brands seeking to capitalize on emerging markets, including strategy, content creation, communications, and media. Unlike traditional agencies, *Flight Story* goes beyond mere outsourcing by integrating its talented team, efficient processes, and cutting-edge technology directly into a company's operations. This unique approach ensures that you have direct access to Flight Story's world-leading global creative and public relations expertise.

In addition to its core services, *Flight Story* is committed to fostering the success of the next generation of European business owners through its *Flight Story Fund*. This innovative initiative brings together the knowledge, resources, and capital of Europe's most accomplished entrepreneurs into a single fund. The aim is to provide invaluable support to aspiring business owners and help them achieve their goals. Furthermore, innovators backed by the Fund will receive personalized assistance in marketing and public relations, ensuring their ventures soar to new heights.

As part of the Flight family, esteemed companies such as R.Agency, Flight Deck, and Flight Performance share the same commitment to excellence and innovation.

The H.S.B

"Happy Sexy Millionaire" was Steven Bartlett's first book, published in 2021. This autobiography chronicles his remarkable journey from being a high school dropout to becoming a multimillionaire. It quickly became a sensation among readers and critics, earning a coveted spot on the Sunday Times bestseller list.

Steven Bartlett's "Happy Sexy Millionaire" is not just another self-help book; it is a captivating guide that leads readers toward fulfillment, accomplishment, and material prosperity. Drawing from his own life experiences and entrepreneurial wisdom, Bartlett provides invaluable advice on achieving success in both personal and professional spheres.

Right from the start, the book challenges conventional notions of success and happiness, encouraging readers to define their own standards. Bartlett emphasizes the importance of cultivating inner contentment and joy, rather than relying solely on external achievements or material possessions. By embracing self-awareness and embracing honesty, readers are inspired to discover their true purpose and create a life that aligns with their core beliefs and aspirations.

In this compelling masterpiece, Bartlett shares his personal triumphs and tribulations, offering practical strategies and insights that can be applied to anyone's life. Through engaging anecdotes and thought-provoking exercises, he empowers readers to overcome obstacles, seize opportunities, and unlock their full potential.

In the pages of *"Happy Sexy Millionaire,"* Bartlett plunges into the transformative power of goal-setting and visualization. He explores practical strategies for defining one's vision, establishing meaningful objectives, and fostering a mindset of abundance and endless possibilities. Through captivating anecdotes and actionable exercises, readers are guided to break free from self-imposed limitations, confront fear and self-doubt head-on, and courageously pursue their dreams.

Beyond the inner journey, Bartlett offers invaluable insights and solutions for attaining wealth and financial independence. He provides practical advice on business, investing, and wealth creation, underscoring the importance of calculated risks and adopting a growth-oriented mindset. Drawing from his own experiences as the founder and former CEO of Social Chain, Bartlett brings an authentic and relevant perspective to his teachings.

This book also digs into the concepts of human responsibility and intentional decision-making. The author emphasizes the importance of taking control of one's choices and embracing the ability to bring about positive change. Readers are encouraged to let go of victimization and adopt an empowering mindset, recognizing their potential to shape their own futures.

Throughout the book, Bartlett sprinkles the narrative with uplifting anecdotes, thought-provoking quotes, and practical examples. His writing style is captivating, realistic, and motivating, making it accessible to individuals from diverse backgrounds and walks of life.

With its inspiring message, practical advice, and profound insights, "Happy Sexy Millionaire" serves as a catalyst for readers to unlock their own potential, attain happiness on their own terms, and construct a life of prosperity and fulfillment.

The Dragons' Den Personality

In 2022, Bartlett became the youngest black investor to join *"Dragons' Den."* A decade before, he was one of the unsuccessful individuals to apply as a contestant on the tv show. This captivating program showcases ambitious entrepreneurs who present their innovative business concepts to a panel of accomplished business moguls. As one of the esteemed dragons, Steven not only offers lucrative investment prospects but also imparts invaluable expertise to aspiring contestants.

In June 2023, Bartlett caused concern among his fans when he posted a message on Instagram implying that it was his last day on the set of the BBC entrepreneur show. In a lengthy post, he expressed his gratitude for the opportunity to be a part of the show and described his experience as a childhood dream come true. He also thanked his fellow dragons, Deborah Meaden, Peter Jones, Sara Davies, and Touker Suleyman for their support and described *Dragons' Den* as an important part of British culture.

However, the post was written in regard to his last day of filming for the current series and not for resignation.

Milestones

Bartlett's career journey has been marked by several important milestones. He began by co-founding *Wallpark*, which later became *Social Chain*, establishing a foundation for his success in digital marketing and social media. Under his leadership, Social Chain experienced rapid growth and expanded internationally, becoming a renowned global social media marketing agency. Bartlett also built a strong personal brand as a social media influencer, sharing insights on entrepreneurship, marketing, and motivation through platforms like YouTube and Instagram Lastly, he expanded his reach by launching the successful podcast, *The Diary Of A CEO*, conducting in-depth interviews with influential figures.

Challenges

Steven Bartlett and Social Chain have successfully overcome various challenges in the marketing and social media industry. Despite fierce competition, they managed to stand out by using innovative strategies, creativity, and data-driven insights to deliver exceptional results. Balancing entrepreneurship and building a personal brand as an influencer required careful time management, which Steven achieved by delegating tasks effectively, surrounding himself with a capable team, and staying disciplined. The digital landscape's constant changes are also a challenge, but Steven and Social Chain embraced agility and adaptability, enabling them to pivot and evolve their strategies to keep up with the evolving social media landscape.

Valuable Contributions

o *Redefining Social Media Marketing:* In order to reach and engage with a younger audience, Steven Bartlett's creative marketing techniques and campaigns helped revolutionize social media marketing. Using a data-driven methodology, Social Chain became an industry leader in influencer marketing.

o *Inspirational Influence:* Many people's aspirations have been sparked, obstacles have been surmounted, and entrepreneurial adventures have been embraced thanks to Steven's inspiring writing and heartfelt stories.

o *Empowering Future Entrepreneurs:*
By building a strong personal brand and maintaining an active online presence, Bartlett has enabled aspiring business owners by sharing his own experiences, both triumphant and humiliating.

o Steven's influence has been felt well beyond the walls of his businesses because to the work he has done in the fields of entrepreneurship and marketing. The community has benefited from his work as a speaker, mentor, and benefactor since he has helped more people reach their full potential.

o To raise awareness and encourage conversation about mental health, Bartlett has been candid about his own experiences with mental illness. He has helped lessen the taboo associated with mental health concerns by speaking openly about his own struggles and inspiring others to do the same.

Bartlett's Inspirational and Motivational Content

Steven Bartlett is well-known for his insightful talks, TED Talks, and interviews on topics such as business, leadership, personal development, and overcoming adversity. He has motivated and uplifted people all around the globe via various mediums. Some notable examples are:

1. In the titled TEDx Talk, *"You Will Never Look at Your Life in the Same Way Again,"* Bartlett gives a stirring

and introspective speech prompting listeners to reconsider their outlook on life. Through anecdotes and reflections, he encourages readers to think outside the box, accept setbacks, and seek meaning in their lives. His speech inspired listeners to abandon their inhibitions and go for their dreams.

2. *The Inspirational Video- "The Fleeting Nature of Time":* In the clip, Steven delivers an inspirational monologue that encourages viewers to live in the now and appreciate time's impermanence. He stresses the value of appreciating the process of living and making the most of every chance.

3. *"How to Win in Life":* On *Impact Theory with Tom Bilyeu,* Steven Bartlett had a conversation with

Bilyeu on the subject *"How to Win in Life."* He spoke about the mentality and behaviors that lead to success in life and business. The proper people, a development mentality, and finding meaning in one's profession were all things he stressed.

4. Instagram and YouTube Content: Our protagonist often share inspirational writeup on his Instagram and YouTube channels, touching on subjects like self-confidence, ambition, and business. These short videos and writeups provide doses of inspiration for his followers.

LESSONS FROM BARTLETT'S EXPERIENCE

Here are a few of the most insightful and thought-provoking quotations and takeaways from Bartlett's inspirational content:

a. *"It's not about where you are; it's about where you're going."*

The takeaway: Never lose sight of your long-term objectives. Your future potential is independent of your present circumstances.

b. *"Embrace failure. It's through failure that we learn the most important lessons."*

Takeaway: Setbacks are opportunities for growth and improvement. Accept failures as stepping stones to self-improvement.

c. *"Success is never owned; it's rented, and the rent is due every day."*

Takeaway: Triumphant experiences stem from constant growth, not a fixed culmination. It calls for persistent work, commitment, and ongoing development.

d. *"Don't let fear dictate your actions. Push past your comfort zone, and amazing things can happen."*

Takeaway: Fear might prevent you from realizing your greatest potential. Opportunity often presents itself to those who are willing to take a few steps beyond their comfort zone and try something new.

e. *"The people you surround yourself with are a reflection of who you are."*

Takeaway: Surround yourself with upbeat, ambitious, and encouraging people who will encourage you to reach your full potential.

f. *"Success is not linear; it's about embracing the highs and lows of the journey."*

Takeaway: The road to success is not without its share of obstacles. Accept the difficulties and revel in the successes.

g. *"Know your 'why.' When you have a strong purpose, you can overcome any 'how.'"*

Takeaway: In order to be persistent and successful, it is important to have a strong will and know why you are working for your objectives.

h. "Your beliefs become your reality..."

Takeaway: Reality is a reflection of your thoughts and attitudes. Develop a confident and self-assured outlook on your talents.

i. "Be adaptable and open to change. The world moves fast, and those who adapt thrive."

Takeaway: The capacity to change and adapt quickly is crucial to success in today's ever-evolving environment.

j. "The journey is just as important as the destination. Enjoy the process and celebrate your growth along the way."

Take pride in learning new things about yourself while growing as a person. Every step of the journey contributes to your personal and professional development.

Tips from Bartlett's Success Strategies

Accept and benefit from setbacks: Every entrepreneur will experience setbacks at some point. Instead of seeing it as a setback, try viewing it as a learning opportunity. Look at the mistakes you've made and learn from them so you can avoid them in the future.

Taking some measured risks is necessary for development and innovation, therefore don't be scared to do so.

Develop a "growth mindset":

The key idea is to develop a mindset focused on growth and constantly learning throughout life. Instead of seeing difficulties as obstacles, perceive them as opportunities to learn and grow. View failures as temporary setbacks on the journey to success and embrace challenges with an open mind, and have confidence in your ability to bounce back.

+ *Define Your Objectives and Visualise Your Success:*

To achieve personal and professional growth, start by defining specific and measurable objectives that are realistic and relevant to you. Set a timeline to accomplish these objectives. In addition, visualize yourself being successful and believe in your abilities. To stay focused and monitor your progress, consider creating a vision board or keeping a diary to track your goals and achievements.

+ *Create a safety net of people who have your back:*

To grow and succeed, it's important to surround yourself with like-minded individuals who share similar values and goals. Building a supportive network of people who can help you in your personal and professional development is key.

One way to benefit from this network is by actively seeking out and listening to the opinions and perspectives of those you trust. Invite them to provide constructive criticism, as this can offer valuable insights and help you learn and improve.

+ *Act Responsible and Take Charge:*

In order to grow and succeed, it is important to acknowledge your achievements and failures by taking full responsibility for your actions. Instead of seeking answers from others, focus on improving what you can control and becoming proficient in those areas.

✦ Concentrate on Your Own Growth:
To constantly improve yourself, prioritize activities such as reading, attending seminars, workshops, or taking online courses. These will help you gain knowledge and skills that align with your personal goals and interests, making you a well-rounded individual.

✦ Strengthen Your Mind and Body for Adversity:
The key to persevering in tough times is to maintain a positive attitude and build resilience, enabling you to continue forward despite difficulties.

✦ *Strive to Find the Sweet Spot Between Ambition and Patience:*
It is important to have ambitious goals and aspirations but also acknowledge that achieving them requires patience and perseverance. This stresses the need to understand that meaningful progress and growth takes time.

✦ *Put your health and mindfulness first:*
It is necessary to treat both your emotional and physical well-being as a priority. This includes getting enough sleep, staying active through exercise, and maintaining other healthy habits. To stay grounded, practice mindfulness and self-awareness to stay present in the current moment.

✦ *Recognize and Honor Even the Most Minimal Accomplishments:*
Recognize and honor your successes, no matter how little they may seem. Do not

fail to appreciate the strides you've made along the road; they add up to getting you closer to your objectives.

PERSONAL LIFE

Bartlett is currently in a committed relationship with Melanie Vaz Lopez, although he generally maintains a discreet approach to his personal life. Nevertheless, avid followers of his highly acclaimed podcast, *Diary of a CEO*, have been fortunate enough to catch glimpses of his romantic involvement. In various episodes, Steven has graciously shared anecdotes about his girlfriend, shedding light on her expertise in the realms of breath work and wellness.

Steven and Melanie embarked on their relationship in 2016, having connected through Instagram. Although they faced a temporary breakup in 2017, destiny brought them back together in 2022. In a captivating interview with Jay Shetty,

Steven openly revealed that his girlfriend had been the driving force behind his newfound dedication to meditation. Recognizing the need to maintain composure and clarity amidst his demanding work schedule, Melanie's influence inspired him to explore the transformative power of meditation.

In a 2017 video on his renowned YouTube channel, Steven, a typically enigmatic figure when it comes to his personal life, candidly unveiled the reasons behind the demise of his previous relationship. He attributed its downfall to the overwhelming demands of his work and business, which consumed the majority of his time. While he fondly described the relationship as extraordinary, he humbly acknowledged that his lack of availability, mental focus, and the constant barrage of distractions ultimately led to its unraveling. Steven confessed that he had become utterly engrossed in his professional endeavors, oblivious to the presence of his loved ones from dawn till dusk. Consequently, he found it nearly impossible to meaningfully connect with his family or girlfriend during that period.

Steven shared his story of trying to win back his ex-girlfriend, Melanie, with podcaster Tolly T. After Melanie went to Bali for a year, he did some soul-searching and realized that he wanted her back. He flew to Bali to apologize to her, and she accepted his apology. While he was there, they stayed friends and met up every other day.

The young *Dragon* revealed that Melanie had surprised him by confessing that she had been involved with someone else during their separation, which he found challenging to come to terms with. However, as a reformed television personality who joined *Dragons Den* in 2021, he asserted that he had dealt with the situation maturely and expressed appreciation for her honesty. Reflecting on his past, he admitted to his immaturity and failure to understand Melanie's discontentment with their initial relationship after a few months in it.

The *Diary of a CEO* host recounts an experience where Melanie made a statement that was confusing which made him feel insecure. She expressed her aversion to sex. He tried to ask for clarification, but his partner refused to discuss it. This caused Steven to end the relationship. However, it turned out that the issue was not about Melanie not liking the act of sex, but rather about communication differences. Upon realizing this, he acknowledged his immaturity and committed to being patient and understanding in order to improve their relationship.

Towards the end of his trip, Steven sent Melanie a heartfelt message expressing his deep gratitude. It was during this exchange that they both realized their love for each other was rekindling. Presently, Steven and Melanie are happily dating and have taken the significant step of moving in together. However, they prefer to keep the intimate details of their relationship private, cherishing their special bond away from prying eyes.

While Steven has mentioned his lack of concern about marriage, he has expressed his desire to have a large family, envisioning a future with six children. On the other hand, Melanie is a successful entrepreneur, running her own beauty and well-being business. Additionally, she is a Reiki Master, bringing healing and balance to those around her.

Fitness and Wellness: Bartlett has stated a desire to be in shape and lead a healthy lifestyle. He thinks that a person's physical health has a direct impact on their ability to think clearly and get things done.

Touring: Like many successful businesspeople and public figures, Steven probably likes taking trips across the world. Because of his international prominence, he probably gets to travel and see other cultures.

Reading: Steven Bartlett is well-known for his devotion to self-improvement via reading. He often promotes reading as an important part of the entrepreneurial process, including book recommendations on his podcast and other social media channels.

Charitable Actions

Giving back to society is something that really matters to Steven Bartlett, and he has made it a focus of his life. He has utilized his fame to bring attention to important social problems and donate to worthy organizations.

Some examples of his commitment to making a difference include:

- He has pushed and brought attention to efforts for social and environmental problems via his social media accounts.

- Advocacy for Mental Health: Steven has spoken publicly about his own experiences with mental illness, and he has used his prominence to normalize conversations about these issues and break down stigma. By discussing his own struggles with mental health, he hopes to inspire others to reach out for assistance when they are in a similar position.

- While some of Steven Bartlett's philanthropic work is publicized via his social media and speaking engagements, some aspects of his giving may be more under the radar.

Awards

Steven Bartlett has been honored for his achievements in business, advertising, and social media. Among the many honors he has already earned up to that moment are the following:

o *Forbes 30 Under 30:* Steven Bartlett earned Forbes's illustrious *"30 Under 30"* list, which honors the most promising young businesspeople and political leaders under the age of 30.

o For his contributions to the business sector and his leadership qualities, Steven was recognized as *"Entrepreneur of the Year"* by a number of institutions and media outlets.

o When compiling their annual *"Digerati"* list honoring the best digital talent and influencers in the UK, *The Drum*, a prominent marketing and media platform, featured Steven Bartlett.

o The Ernst & Young Entrepreneur of the Year Award is a prestigious honor given annually to a business leader who has shown extraordinary entrepreneurial qualities such as invention, growth, and leadership. This honor was bestowed on Steven in acknowledgment of his significant contributions to the field of marketing.

o Steven was honored as *"Young Entrepreneur of the Year"* by *Startups.co.uk,* a website dedicated to supporting new businesses, for his many successes and noteworthy contributions to the business world at such a young age.

o For his contributions to the local business community, Steven and Social Chain were honored at the Manchester Evening News Business Awards.

o The 2017 Year's Most Powerful Agency Head: According to the 2017 Econsultancy's Top 100 Digital Agencies Report, Steven Bartlett was the most important agency personality. This recognition is a tribute to his leadership and pioneering spirit in the field of digital marketing.

o The Entrepreneur of the Year award in Great Britain for 2019 settled on Steven Bartlett. This honor is in appreciation of his success as a young business leader and his impact on the economy of the United Kingdom.

SUMMARY

British businessman, social media sensation, and motivational speaker, Steven Cliff Bartlett, has made a significant impact in the realms of marketing and entrepreneurship. Bartlett's early life was shaped by his family background and upbringing in Botswana, Africa, where he was born and raised. Eventually, he found his way to the United Kingdom, where he pursued further education and embarked on an impressive professional journey.

Upon completing his education, Bartlett fearlessly plunged into the world of business, launching multiple successful ventures even as a teenager. In 2012, he co-founded *Wallpark*, which has evolved into the renowned *Social Chain*, an international powerhouse in social media advertising. Under Bartlett's visionary leadership, Social Chain has thrived, gaining recognition for its cutting-edge advertising strategies and its ability to resonate with the younger generation.

Steven overcame numerous obstacles in his professional journey through his unwavering flexibility and persistence. He cultivated a growth mindset that enabled him to perceive setbacks as valuable opportunities for self-improvement. Through his captivating TED Talks, enlightening podcasts, and insightful interviews, Steven has become a beacon of motivation and inspiration for aspiring entrepreneurs and enthusiasts worldwide. Beyond his professional endeavors, Bartlett nurtures a diverse range of interests. He dedicates himself to maintaining physical fitness, embarking on exciting adventures to explore new places, and constantly expanding his knowledge base. Leveraging his influential status, he utilizes his platform to champion social causes, advocate for improved mental health care, and actively contribute to the betterment of society.

The marketing and entrepreneurship communities have greatly benefited from the contributions of Steven Bartlett. His exceptional work has earned him numerous accolades, such as Entrepreneur of the Year and Ernst & Young Entrepreneur of the Year, and he has been featured on prestigious lists like Forbes 30 Under 30.

The ascent of Bartlett, from a teenage entrepreneur to a prominent corporate leader, serves as an inspiring example. Through his determination, integrity, and dedication to personal growth, he has established himself as a prominent figure in the realms of business and social media marketing.

Printed in Great Britain
by Amazon

38455675R00051